Teachers, librarians, and kids
from across Canada are talking about
Canadian Flyer Adventures.
Here's what some of them had to say:

Great Canadian historical content, excellent illustrations,
and superb closing historical facts (I love the kids'
commentary!). ~ *SARA S., TEACHER, ONTARIO*

As a teacher–librarian I welcome this series with open
arms. It fills the gap for Canadian historical adventures
at an early reading level! There's fast action, interesting,
believable characters, and great historical information.
~ *MARGARET L., TEACHER–LIBRARIAN, BRITISH COLUMBIA*

The *Canadian Flyer Adventures* will transport young
readers to different eras of our past with their appealing
topics. Thank goodness there are more artifacts in that old
dresser ... they are sure to lead to even more escapades.
~ *SALLY B., TEACHER–LIBRARIAN, MANITOBA*

When I shared the book with a grade 1–2 teacher at
my school, she enjoyed the book, noting that her students
would find it appealing because of the action-adventure
and short chapters. ~ *HEATHER J., TEACHER AND
LIBRARIAN, NOVA SCOTIA*

Newly independent readers will fly through
each *Canadian Flyer Adventure*, and be asking for
the next installment! Children will enjoy the fast-paced
narrative, the personalities of the main characters, and
the drama of the dangerous situations the children
find themselves in. ~ *PAM L., LIBRARIAN, ONTARIO*

I love the fact that these are Canadian adventures—kids should know how exciting Canadian history is. Emily and Matt are regular kids, full of curiosity, and I can see readers relating to them. ~ *JEAN K., TEACHER, ONTARIO*

What kids told us:

I would like to have the chance to ride on a magical sled and have adventures. ~ *EMMANUEL*

I would like to tell the author that her book is amazing, incredible, awesome, and a million times better than any book I've read. ~ *MARIA*

I would recommend the *Canadian Flyer Adventures* series to other kids so they could learn about Canada too. The book is just the right length and hard to put down. ~ *PAUL*

The books I usually read are the full-of-fact encyclopedias. This book is full of interesting ideas that simply grab me. ~ *ELEANOR*

At the end of the book Matt and Emily say they are going on another adventure. I'm very interested in where they are going next! ~ *ALEX*

I like when Emily and Matt fly into the sky on a sled towards a new adventure. I can't wait for the next book! ~ *JI SANG*

Crazy for Gold

Frieda Wishinsky

Illustrated by Dean Griffiths

MAPLE
TREE

Maple Tree is an imprint of Owlkids Books Inc.
10 Lower Spadina Avenue, Suite 400, Toronto, Ontario M5V 2Z2
www.owlkidsbooks.com

Text © 2007 Frieda Wishinsky   Illustrations © 2007 Dean Griffiths

Distributed in Canada by University of Toronto Press
5201 Dufferin Street, Toronto, Ontario M3H 5T8

Distributed in the United States by Publishers Group West
1700 Fourth Street, Berkeley, California 94710

Dedication
With love to Tatiana

Acknowledgements
Many thanks to the hard-working Maple Tree team—Sheba Meland, Anne Shone,
Ann Featherstone, Grenfell Featherstone, Deborah Bjorgan, Cali Hoffman, Erin Walker, and Dawn
Todd—for their insightful comments and steadfast support. Special thanks to Dean Griffiths and
Claudia Dávila for their engaging and energetic illustrations and design.

Cataloguing in Publication Data
Wishinsky, Frieda
Crazy for gold / Frieda Wishinsky ; illustrated by Dean Griffiths.

(Canadian flyer adventures ; 3)
ISBN-13: 978-1-897066-92-8 (bound) / ISBN-10: 1-897066-92-9 (bound)
ISBN-13: 978-1-897066-93-5 (pbk.) / ISBN-10: 1-897066-93-7 (pbk.)

1. Klondike River Valley (Yukon)—Gold discoveries—Juvenile fiction.
I. Griffiths, Dean, 1967– II. Title. III. Series: Wishinsky, Frieda. Canadian flyer adventures ; 3.

PS8595.I834C73 2007   jC813'.54   C2006-904158-X

Design & art direction: Claudia Dávila

Canadian   Patrimoine
Heritage   canadien

Canada Council   Conseil des Arts
for the Arts   du Canada

Canadä

ONTARIO ARTS COUNCIL
CONSEIL DES ARTS DE L'ONTARIO

Ontario

Ontario Media Development
Corporation
Société de développement
de l'industrie des médias
de l'Ontario

We acknowledge the financial support of the Canada Council for the Arts, the Ontario Arts Council,
the Government of Canada through the Canada Book Fund (CBF) and the Government of Ontario
through the Ontario Media Development Corporation's Book Initiative for our publishing activities.

Printed in Canada

B   C   D   E   F

CONTENTS

HOW IT ALL BEGAN

Emily and Matt couldn't believe their luck. They discovered an old dresser full of strange objects in the tower of Emily's house. They also found a note from Emily's Great-Aunt Miranda: "The sled is yours. Fly it to wonderful adventures."

They found a sled right behind the dresser! When they sat on it, shimmery gold words appeared:

> *Rub the leaf*
> *Three times fast.*
> *Soon you'll fly*
> *To the past.*

The sled rose over Emily's house. It flew over their town of Glenwood. It sailed out of a cloud and into the past. Their adventures on the flying sled had begun! Where will the sled take them next? Turn the page to find out.

1

To the Tower

Emily stared out the living room window. Why did it have to rain on Saturday? It had rained all morning. Now it was twelve o'clock and it was still raining. When would it stop?

Maybe I'll call Matt, she thought. *Maybe we can—*

And then she saw him. He was carrying a black umbrella. He was walking to her house. Before he could ring the bell, she opened the door.

"Let's go on an adventure," she said.

Matt grinned. "Where do you want to go this time?"

"Follow me to the tower and you'll see," said Emily.

Matt and Emily raced up the rickety steps to the tower. As soon as they were inside, she opened the second drawer of the dresser and pulled out a wide-brimmed brown leather hat. It was labelled *Gold Rush, 1898*.

Emily popped the hat on her head. It was so big, it covered her eyes. "Remember that movie about the kids who ran away to join their father in the Klondike Gold Rush?" she asked.

Matt nodded. They'd seen that movie last Saturday.

"Remember how they were the only ones to find gold near Dawson City? If the magic sled takes us there, I bet we could find gold!"

"Great!" exclaimed Matt.

Emily slipped the hat off and put it back in the drawer. "I have my sketchbook." She patted the pocket of her blue jeans. "I'm going to draw us with pockets full of gold."

"And I'm going to use my digital recorder to tell how we find the gold," said Matt.

"So what are we waiting for? Let's go!"

Emily and Matt hopped on the *Canadian Flyer*.

Immediately, shimmery gold words appeared.

Rub the leaf
Three times fast.
Soon you'll fly
To the past.

"Gold rush, here we come!" sang Emily, rubbing the maple leaf at the front of the sled.

2
Cold Rush

All they could see was white. All they could feel was cold.

"What kind of gold rush is this? It's freezing," said Emily, shivering.

"It's a *cold* rush," said Matt through chattering teeth. "At least we're dressed in warm clothes. Look at these outfits!"

Matt was wearing heavy brown pants, a brown shirt, a woollen jacket, a hat with ear flaps, heavy black boots, and mittens. Emily wore a long, navy blue dress, a blue coat with a hood, thick blue stockings, high lace-up black boots, and mittens.

As the sled flew lower, thick snowflakes filled the air like confetti.

"Yikes! We're in a blizzard!" shouted Emily.

They were covered in snow. Everything was so white, they couldn't see ahead or behind them. A sharp wind swirled snow into their eyes.

With a thud, the sled landed on ice. As they scrambled off, Emily stumbled. She tripped on something hard and lumpy.

"Get off my foot!" someone yelled.

Emily moved her foot and looked up.

A girl of about ten with long brown braids was glaring at her. The girl was wearing a thick tweed coat and brown boots.

"Is that better?" Emily asked.

"Much better," said the girl. "Who are you?"

"I'm Emily Bing, and this is Matt Martinez."

"My name is Isabel Langley," said the girl. "Are you new here? I've never seen you before."

Emily looked at Matt. How could they explain that they had flown here on a magic sled from the future?

But they had to tell Isabel something. And that's when Emily remembered the gold rush movie.

"We're on our own," Emily blurted out. "We ran away to find my dad. He joined the gold rush."

"Why did you run away?" asked Isabel.

"We had to," Matt chimed in. "We were staying with my mean Uncle Burt. He made us sleep in a dark basement."

Phew! Matt remembers the movie, too, thought Emily.

"That must have been terrible," said Isabel. "I hope you find your father soon."

Emily wished they didn't have to make up a story, but how else could they explain how they'd landed here? Emily glanced at the snow-covered tents, the sleds loaded with supplies, and the people tramping up a steep mountain trail. Where was *here* anyway? It looked like nowhere.

"When are you climbing the Golden Stairs up the Chilkoot Pass?" asked Isabel. She pointed to the mountain trail.

"I don't know," said Emily. "But that's a weird name for stairs. They don't look like gold."

Isabel laughed. "I know. They're just stairs carved into the ice. You have to climb them to get to the summit of the pass. From there, you can go on to Dawson City in the Yukon. That's where my papa is looking for gold. Is your papa there, too?"

"We're n-not sure wh-where he is," stammered Matt. Emily knew Matt wasn't feeling good about making up a story, either. She hoped Isabel wouldn't ask them any more questions.

"I'm travelling with my mama," Isabel said. "She didn't want to come, but Papa is crazy for gold like your papa. We've camped here for months. But we're finally ready to go to Dawson City."

"How far is it from here?" asked Matt.

"Hundreds of miles away," said Isabel.

"Oh no," groaned Matt. It was going to take a lot longer than he thought to find gold.

"Maybe you could travel with us," suggested Isabel. "It would be fun to travel together. You're the only people my age I've met here."

"Sure!" agreed Matt and Emily.

"There's Mama," said Isabel. She pointed to a short, stocky woman beside a man wearing a wide-brimmed brown hat. It was a hat just like the one they had seen in the dresser!

"Mama's giving some of her sourdough biscuits to Mr. Roberts and his three sons. They're helping us bring our supplies over the pass. They love her biscuits."

"Sourdough biscuits!" exclaimed Emily. The kids in the movie loved them, too. And Emily was hungry. They'd been so excited to start their new adventure that they had forgotten all about lunch.

"Mama brought the sourdough starter from California," Isabel explained. "That way we can always make fresh biscuits. She made a batch in our camp stove before the blizzard this morning. If you're hungry, I can ask her if she has extra."

"We're starving," said Matt.

"Wait here," said Isabel. "I'll ask Mama if you can have some biscuits and if you can go to Dawson with us. Oh, I hope she says yes!"

3

Icy Stairs

As Isabel raced off to speak to her mother, Matt pulled out his recorder. "This is Matt reporting. Emily and I are on our way to Dawson City to find gold. But first we have to climb steep, icy steps called the Golden Stairs to get to the summit of the pass. Will we make it to the top? Will we find gold? Stay tuned."

"Isabel's coming," said Emily. "Hurry! Shut the recorder off."

Matt quickly shoved it into his pocket just as Isabel ran over.

She was beaming. "Mama said you can travel with us! I've missed having friends my age so much. But now you're here. Now everything will be different!"

"That's great!" said Matt. He was glad that he and Emily wouldn't be travelling alone. Finding gold was going to be a lot harder and colder than he imagined.

"When do we start climbing?" Emily asked.

"I'll ask Mama. Here she comes," said Isabel.

Mrs. Langley tramped toward them through the knee-high snow. "So you're the children Isabel has been telling me about. I hear you're hungry. Would you like some biscuits?"

"Thank you," said Matt and Emily. The biscuits were crunchy on the outside and chewy on the inside.

"Mmm," said Emily. "These are delicious!"

"I told you my mama makes the best sour-dough biscuits in the world," said Isabel.

Mrs. Langley smiled but her eyes looked tired.

"Let's all have a hot drink before we start climbing," she said. "We'll need all our strength to haul the last of our supplies to the top." She pointed to the side of the trail.

Piles of abandoned wagons, rusty trunks, and broken sleds lay on the ground. A bony, panting horse wandered about.

"Poor horse," said Emily.

"This trail is tough, not just on people," said Mrs. Langley. "We're lucky that Mr. Roberts and his boys helped us haul most of our supplies up the pass already. They've begun their last climb. Thank goodness it's also our last trip up those miserable Golden Stairs."

"You mean you've gone to the top before?" asked Matt.

"I've been up and down forty times. Isabel made it to the top twice."

Matt shivered. "How did you get up there even once?"

"It's hard on the way up," explained Isabel. "But on the way down, you slide on your rump. You're back in no time!"

"Why did you have go up so many times?" asked Emily.

"We brought a lot of supplies," answered Mrs. Langley. "The North West Mounted Police won't let anyone go to Dawson without a year's worth of food and equipment. They don't want people starving or freezing to death."

"We don't have supplies," said Matt. "We don't have anything except our sled."

"Don't worry," Mrs. Langley assured them. "We've brought enough. And you can help haul up our last loads. We'll tell the police you're with us—that you're part of our family. Here. You'll need these, too." She gave each of the children a wooden climbing stick.

Matt wrapped their sled and two packs of flour in one of Mrs. Langley's blankets. Emily helped him strap the sled to his back with rope.

"I wish the sled could fly us up that mountain," she whispered to Matt.

"Can you imagine the looks we'd get if it did *that?*" he said as he helped Emily strap on sacks of beans and dried vegetables. Then he helped Isabel strap on a pack of food while Mrs. Langley wrapped their small stove in canvas and hoisted it on her own back.

"Let's climb!" she said.

4

Up the Golden Stairs

Mrs. Langley led the way, followed by Matt, Emily, and Isabel. As they climbed, they held on to the icy rope leading up to the summit. They dug their sticks into each slippery, frozen step.

An hour passed. Two hours. Three.

Emily felt as if she'd been climbing for days. Her arms and legs ached. Her eyes stung from the blowing snow. Her throat hurt from the cold air.

She glanced back at the long line of people

trudging behind them. Everyone was hunched over from the weight of their packs and the stinging wind. Everyone looked like they were dragging themselves to the summit. But no one stopped moving.

And then she heard a cry. "Help! Please!"

It was Isabel! She lay in a heap two steps below. Her climbing stick lay broken beside her.

The line had stopped moving as people waited for her to get up. Matt, Emily, and Mrs. Langley hurried down. Isabel's leg was twisted under her.

"It's my ankle," Isabel groaned.

Mrs. Langley examined Isabel's ankle. "I don't think it's broken," she said. "Can you walk?"

"I think so," said Isabel. She held on to her mother's arm and tried to stand up. "I just don't know if I can make it to the top."

"You can," said Emily. "Use my climbing stick."

"Thanks," said Isabel. As she struggled to climb the next step, she winced in pain. But she kept moving.

If only we could rest, thought Emily. But she knew they couldn't—not with an army of people moving behind them. They just had to keep climbing.

More hours passed. Emily's feet and fingers were numb with cold. Each step hurt. Each breath made her chest ache. When would they ever reach the summit?

But finally she saw it. It was only steps away.

As they neared the top, the wind blew so fiercely that Emily was sure it would lift her up like a pebble and toss her off the mountain.

She looked at Isabel. Her friend's eyelashes

were thick with snow. Tears rolled down her cheeks. "I don't think I can walk another step," Isabel moaned.

"We're almost there," said Emily. "You can make it. I know you can."

"I'll try," Isabel whispered.

Matt began to count. "Five. Four. Three. Two. One. I made it!" He waved his climbing stick in the air like a trophy.

"Me, too!" shouted Emily.

"Me, three!" shouted Isabel.

5

On Top

The children sank down in the snow. They unstrapped their packs and stretched their aching legs.

"Whoever called these stairs *golden* is crazy," said Emily.

"But we did it! We climbed every step!" said Isabel. She smiled for the first time since they began their trek.

"My back feels like it's on fire," said Matt. "That sled is heavy when you're carrying it up a gazillion steps."

"There weren't *that* many," said Emily.

"Maybe not, but it felt like it."

"You did well, children," said Mrs. Langley. "And I checked the supplies we brought up earlier. Our packs are covered with snow, but they're all here!"

The children followed Mrs. Langley to a long-handled shovel sticking out of the snow to mark their packs. Mrs. Langley had tied a red

bandana to the top of it. It flapped like a kite in the wind.

Emily peered at the hundreds of weary people who'd made it to the summit. Some were huddled inside their mud-stained tents. Others leaned against their snow-covered packs. It looked like a city of dirty, tattered tents. Dawson City had to be better than this miserable place!

"After a hot drink and a biscuit, we'll pay our tolls to the Mounted Police and be off," Mrs. Langley told them.

"Please. Can't we rest here a little longer?" pleaded Isabel, rubbing her sore ankle. "My ankle still hurts."

"I'll wrap it to ease the pain," said Mrs. Langley. "But we have to keep going. We have to reach Crater Lake today. We'll make good time with our sleds, but we need to set up our tents before dark."

"Where do we go after Crater Lake?" asked Emily.

"We have to sled our supplies to Lake Bennett," explained Mrs. Langley. "And we'll have to travel back and forth a few times. But once everything's moved, we'll be ready to sail! The Roberts will build a boat and we'll all sail it to the Yukon River. The river will carry us to Dawson."

Emily sighed. She couldn't imagine how they could walk or sled any farther. They were all so tired. Still, they'd come all this way to find gold and they would!

Mrs. Langley fired up the small stove she'd placed on a patch of ground. She put a kettle on for tea.

As they sipped their warm drinks, they saw a skinny, sandy-haired boy of about twelve, asleep against his ripped pack. A bag of dried beans spilled out of one end of the pack. The boy looked hungry and alone. Mrs. Langley walked over and left some biscuits on a faded blue and yellow scarf that lay beside him.

"Poor boy," she said. "At least he'll have something to eat when he wakes up."

Emily looked around. Most people looked as tired and miserable as the boy. Most looked like they didn't want to take another step—anywhere.

6

The River

After a quick meal, they began to sled their supplies toward Crater Lake. Before dark, they had their tents set up. Mrs. Langley cooked bean soup and baked biscuits for supper. Then everyone went to bed.

"I could sleep for a week," said Matt, sliding into the bedroll Mrs. Langley had given him.

"I could sleep for a year," said Emily yawning. "What about you, Isabel?"

But Isabel said nothing. She was sound asleep already.

The next day the children woke up stiff and hungry.

"How's your ankle?" Emily asked Isabel.

"Better but it still hurts."

"Don't worry," said Emily. "We'll pull you on our sled."

"Thank you, children," said Mrs. Langley. "You have been so kind to Isabel. And just think, in only a few days, we'll reach Lake Bennett. Then we'll really be on our way!"

"A few more days *just* to get to Lake Bennett," Matt whispered to Emily. "This is not a gold rush. It's a *slow* rush."

"Finding gold looked like a lot more fun in the movies," said Emily.

For the next week, they sledded their supplies. Finally everything was moved to Lake Bennett.

"At least now we can build our boat," said Emily that night, as they got ready for bed. "I can't wait to sail on a beautiful lake instead of sledding over bumpy ground."

The next day, Mr. Roberts and his three sons began to build the boat. They worked day and night. They cut down trees, lugged wood through the forest, sawed, hammered, and nailed together their flat-bottomed boat, which they called a scow. Mrs Langley sewed sails out of canvas.

"What should we name our boat?" she asked the children.

"*Gold Dust*," said Isabel.

"*Dawson City Here We Come*," suggested Emily.

"*Almost There*," said Matt.

Everyone liked Matt's name the best. So Mrs. Langley embroidered the words on a sail.

While the *Almost There* was being built, the children helped prepare food and run errands. They even knocked in some nails. When they finished their chores, they invented games, slid down hills, and told each other scary stories.

It was late May. The weather was getting warmer and the days were getting longer. It was hardly ever dark now.

"Thanks to this land of the midnight sun, we have more daylight to work on our boat," said Mr. Roberts. "It's almost finished! Come see it!"

They all ran to the shore.

As Isabel and Matt climbed into the scow, Emily perched on a log. She pulled out her sketchbook and drew the *Almost There* and some of the other boats. They were all funny-looking. Some looked like floating bathtubs. Others looked like coffins.

Emily couldn't believe that such weird-looking boats could make it all the way to Dawson. Even their scow looked wobbly but Mr. Roberts swore it could withstand anything, even the rapids.

"We're from Seattle," he said proudly. "We know how to build boats and sail them."

"I hope so," Emily whispered to Matt. "I don't want to swim to Dawson."

Two days later, their boat was ready.

"Tomorrow," said Mr. Roberts, "we sail."

The hard part of the gold rush is finally over, thought Emily. The easy, fun part is starting!

The next morning, Emily crawled out of her bedroll and peeked out of the tent. Mrs. Langley and Isabel were cooking a breakfast of porridge.

Emily tapped Matt on the shoulder. "Matt, wake up."

"Go away," he grumbled.

"But we're leaving soon."

Isabel lifted the tent flap. "Breakfast is ready," she announced.

Isabel's eyes sparkled with excitement. "Soon we'll be in Dawson! I can't wait to see Papa and Dawson and everything!"

"If Matt doesn't get up soon, he won't see Dawson or anything," said Emily.

"Hold your horses," murmured Matt. "I'll be right there."

Emily followed Isabel outside. They drank hot tea and ate a bowl of porridge with sugar. Then they packed up their clothes and food. When Matt joined them, he helped roll up the tents.

"Let's go!" said Mrs. Langley.

They hurried to the busy shore of Lake Bennett.

The *Almost There* was bobbing in the water beside hundreds of other boats. People were shouting, laughing, calling—even singing. For the first time since they'd joined the gold rush,

Emily felt excitement in the air. Dawson was just a boat ride away!

"All aboard!" boomed Mr. Roberts. They loaded the last of their supplies and the sled on the boat and scrambled on.

Eric, Mr. Roberts' oldest son, pushed their boat into the mint-green water. Then he jumped on and began to row. They were off!

Lake Bennett was as calm as a swimming hole. It was speckled with boats of every size, colour, and shape.

"Look! There's a robin!" called Matt, pointing to the shore.

"I see geese," said Emily.

"Hurray! We're on our way!" sang Isabel.

"And we only have 500 miles to go," said Mrs. Langley, laughing.

For a few hours, they rowed down the lake. Sometimes they caught a breeze and they sailed through the water.

"This lake is just like a big bathtub!" said Emily.

"Not for long," said Mr. Roberts. "Listen!"

A loud rumble filled the air.

"Is that thunder?" asked Matt.

"No," said Mr. Roberts. "It's the Yukon River rapids. We're heading into Miles Canyon. Hold on tight, folks. We're in for a bumpy ride!"

7

Wild Water

Bubbling, churning water smashed against the *Almost There*. It rose and fell like a roller coaster.

Emily's stomach lurched with each wave. *I can't be sick,* she told herself. She stared at the horizon as Mr. Roberts had told them so they wouldn't feel queasy. But it was hard not to throw up. One look at Matt and Isabel's face told her they felt the same.

Emily watched in horror as a boat beside them hit a rock and almost tipped over.

The four passengers stayed aboard, but all their goods tumbled into the rock-filled water.

And then as suddenly as they'd entered, the boat was out of the rapids.

"Yahoo!" shouted Emily. "We made it!"

"There's more," said Mr. Roberts. "We're through Miles Canyon, but the Squaw and White Horse Rapids are coming up."

Matt gulped. "More rapids? Wh-when?"

"Soon," said Eric.

"Now!" shouted Emily. "Look!"

Jagged rocks jutted out of the swirling river. Water boiled up from the depths of the canyon.

Mr. Roberts yelled for everyone to hold tight to the sides of the boat. "I'll get you through this," he promised. He steered the *Almost There* between the sharp rocks and logs. Nothing and no one fell over the edge.

Others weren't so lucky. Emily, Matt, and Isabel stared at the wreckage of boats smashed into pieces by the rapids. They saw men lying on the shore drenched and moaning. Others just stared blankly at the water that had swallowed up their belongings and their boats.

Mr. Roberts steered them through the last of the rapids. Then they headed for shore to camp for the night.

As Mrs. Langley cooked them a hot supper of thick soup, a tall, broad-chested man strode over.

"I'm Samuel Steele," he told them. "Superintendent of the North West Mounted Police. You folks were lucky. Many people didn't make it today."

"I've run rapids before," said Mr. Roberts.

"You're one of the few," said Superintendent Steele. "We lost five people in the water and

150 boats today. I am no longer permitting women, children, or inexperienced sailors to run the rapids. Too many have died."

"Is it easy sailing from here?" asked Matt.

"Well, as long as the mosquitoes don't eat you alive, you'll be fine," said Mr. Steele. Then he bid them goodnight and walked off.

8

Where's the Gold?

"I hate sun!" grumbled Emily. She wiped her sweaty face with her sleeve.

"I hate mosquitoes!" said Matt. He slapped one as it stung his neck.

"I hate gnats and blackflies!" cried Isabel. She scratched her legs. They were spotted with swollen, red bites.

"Just a little longer, children," said Mrs. Langley. "We'll be in Dawson soon."

"I hope so," said Eric Roberts. "These mosquitoes are as fat as pigs."

"And as hungry," said Len Roberts. He smacked two that were feasting on his ear.

Luckily, they'd brought a roll of net mesh to keep the bugs away at night. But not everyone sailing to Dawson brought mesh. All night people swatted and cursed the Yukon bugs.

Just as Mrs. Langley had said, it was still 500 miles to Dawson. They were slowly getting closer and closer. A few days later, after they rounded a rocky bluff, they finally saw it. Only it wasn't the city any of them had imagined.

Emily and Matt gaped at the jumble of dusty tents, half-finished buildings, warehouses, and muddy streets. They stared at the weary, dazed people shuffling through the city.

"This is Dawson?" said Matt. "It looks..."

"Ugly," said Emily. "I can't believe there's gold in *this* muddy place."

"Where's Papa?" Isabel asked her mother.

"He lives out of the city," said Mrs. Langley. She peered at the crowds walking up and down the main street. "He'll be here soon. He said he'd look for us every day until we arrived."

"Well, folks," said Mr. Roberts, tying up their boat. "This is where we say goodbye, at least for now. I am sure we will meet up again here in Dawson."

"I can't thank you enough for all your help," said Mrs. Langley. "We couldn't have managed without you."

"Glad to have been of assistance. And glad to have the company of such a fine group," said Mr. Roberts.

Mr. Roberts and his sons waved goodbye. Then they hurried down the street.

As soon as they left, a scruffy, bearded man in faded overalls approached them. "Isabel? Molly?" he said.

"Henry!" shouted Mrs. Langley, hugging her husband.

"Papa!" shouted Isabel, hugging him, too.

Mrs. Langley introduced Emily and Matt. She told her husband that they were looking for Emily's father. She said they'd been a big help on the long trip.

"You can stay with us until you find him," said Mr. Langley.

Emily and Matt looked at each other. Emily knew what Matt was thinking. She was thinking it, too. Who'd want to stay in this ramshackle, run-down city—even if it was dripping with gold?

9

Gold!

Everyone climbed into the rickety wagon
Mr. Langley had borrowed to drive them to his
cabin.

"Giddy-up," he said to the scrawny black
horse pulling the wagon.

It was nearly midnight when the late
northern sun began to set. They finally stopped
in front of a small log cabin.

"Welcome," said Mr. Langley.

The cabin had three cramped rooms, a table
with four lopsided wooden stools, and four

shelves nailed to the walls.

As they stored their packs and sleds behind the cabin, Emily saw Mrs. Langley bite her lip. She looked like she was trying not to cry.

"I know this cabin isn't much," said Mr. Langley. "Every nail and piece of glass costs so much here."

"It's much nicer than our tent," said Isabel, putting her arms around her father.

"And there are no mosquitoes in here," said Matt.

"Except for one." Emily swatted a mosquito on her arm. "But I got him!"

Everyone laughed for the first time since they'd reached the cabin.

"We all figured we'd just dip our hands into a stream and scoop up buckets of gold," Mr. Langley explained. "That's not the way things have turned out."

Mr. Langley told them how many of the gold stakes had already been claimed before he arrived. He'd claimed the stream behind the cabin and panned it for gold. But he found nothing. All he could do now was mine for gold deep in the bedrock. He described the back-breaking work of digging in hard rock and finding only gold dust.

"I've thought about coming home a thousand times," he said. "But I kept hoping things would get better—that my luck would change."

Mrs. Langley wrapped her arms around her husband. "We'll just have to make do," she said. "Come, dear. Let's fire up the stove and I'll bake your favourite biscuits."

Mr. Langley's face brightened. "How I've missed your baking. No one bakes like you, Molly."

Emily, Isabel, and Matt helped Mrs. Langley

make biscuits and soup. Soon, a warm, sweet smell filled the drab cabin. They all sat down to supper. It was nearly 1:30 a.m. when they finished eating and headed off to bed.

Early the next morning, the sun streamed through the cabin's two small windows. Emily woke up and looked around. Everyone was still asleep. She slid out of her bedroll, got dressed, and tiptoed outside.

Although the ground was muddy, pink and yellow wildflowers bloomed everywhere. She sat on a damp log and drew a picture of the cabin and a bird in a tree.

"Hi, Em!" Matt slid in beside her. "What do you want to do now?"

"Look for gold, of course."

"But you heard Mr. Langley. There isn't much around."

"We still might find some. I'm good at finding things. I found my mom's keys after she looked everywhere. Maybe we can find some gold in the stream over there."

"Gold is harder to find than keys," said Matt. "And Mr. Langley panned there already."

"Oh, come on. Let's look anyway. You never know."

Matt sighed. "Okay. Race you to the stream."

Emily and Matt grabbed a couple of pans beside the cabin door. They ran to the stream. They made it to the edge at the same time. "Tie!" they sang, laughing. They slipped off their boots and waded into the stream. It was rocky and muddy. They scooped handfuls of sand and swirled it around the pan, peering inside for nuggets of gold. But there was nothing. Not even a fleck.

"I knew it. Nothing," said Matt.

"Nothing, *yet*," said Emily.

They scooped some more. Still nothing.

"I'm tired," said Matt. "All this panning is making me hungry. Let's go back."

"Come on," said Emily. "Let's check out one more place over there." She pointed to a small pool of water beside a large rock.

"You check," said Matt. "I'm going back. I bet Mrs. Langley is starting to make breakfast. Maybe she's even baking those scrumptious biscuits."

Matt turned to go.

"Matt!" screamed Emily. "Come here! Look what I've found!"

Matt ran back. Emily was holding a small canvas bag. "It was in a hole in the rock," she said. "It's not even wet."

Emily opened the bag. It was full of tiny gold nuggets. There was also a folded note.

"Wow!" said Matt. "What does the note say?"

Emily unfolded it and read aloud.

To whomever finds this bag:
This is for you! I found gold. Lots of it. More than enough for one person. I'm heading home now. I've had enough of this miserable place. I hope this gold brings you good luck. You'll need it!
P.D.

"Hurray!" shouted Emily, jumping up and down in the stream.

"Stop jumping!" said Matt. "You're getting me all wet."

"Who cares!" said Emily. "We found gold!"

Matt laughed. "I know." He turned on his recorder. "Breaking news! After climbing icy trails, sailing down wild rapids, sweating in the hot sun, and getting bitten by hungry mosquitoes, we finally found gold!"

"Come on," said Emily. "Let's show the Langleys."

Matt snapped off his recorder. They hurried out of the stream.

Emily placed the bag of gold on the ground. Then she and Matt wiped their feet on the grass and put on their boots. But before she could pick the bag up again, someone grabbed it.

"Stop!" cried Emily.

But the thief wouldn't stop.

10

For You

The thief was a boy! He had sandy hair and looked about twelve. He ran toward the woods behind the Langley's cabin.

Matt and Emily raced after him, but he was taller and faster than they were.

And then he tripped on the *Canadian Flyer*. The canvas bag flew out of his hands.

He sprawled on the ground, clutching his leg and moaning. Gold nuggets lay scattered all around him.

"Stupid sled," the boy muttered.

His pants and shirt were full of holes. The only thing that wasn't in tatters was a blue and yellow scarf around his neck.

"I've seen you before," said Emily, as she and Matt picked up the nuggets.

"I've never seen you," muttered the boy.

"I know! You're the boy we saw at the summit of the Chilkoot Pass," said Emily. "I remember that scarf."

"It was my dad's scarf," moaned the boy.

"And you're the boy Mrs. Langley left the biscuits for!" said Matt.

"Those biscuits were good," said the boy. "I hadn't eaten anything except beans in two days."

The boy tried to stand up, but his leg buckled under him.

Matt offered his hand.

"Thanks," mumbled the boy.

"What's your name?" asked Emily as they helped him up.

"Dan." He grimaced as he took a step.

"I'm Emily, and this is Matt. We're with the Langleys. They live in this cabin."

"Where's your family?" asked Matt.

"I have no family. My dad died on the trail." Tears sprang into Dan's eyes. Quickly he wiped them away with his sleeve. "I've never stolen anything before. I'm hungry."

"Mrs. Langley will give you some food," said Matt.

"Why are you helping me?" asked Dan. "I stole your gold."

"You *almost* stole our gold," Emily corrected him.

"And you stole so you could eat," said Matt.

As they opened the cabin door, they could smell butter and cinnamon. Mrs. Langley was pulling a pan of cinnamon buns out of the stove.

"Who's this?" she asked as they helped Dan onto a stool.

The children told the Langleys what had happened. They explained how they'd found a bag of gold nuggets and how Dan must have been watching, and grabbed it. They said he was hungry and alone.

"I'm sorry I took the gold," said Dan. "But my father took sick before we reached the summit of the Chilkoot. I buried him. After that, I lost most of my supplies in the blizzard."

"That blizzard was terrible," said Isabel.

"How did the Mounted Police let you over the pass by yourself and without supplies?" asked Matt.

"I snuck in behind a family," Dan explained. "I figured that if I went to Dawson, maybe I would find gold. Or a job. But it's hard to find anything here."

"I know," said Mr. Langley. "To tell you the truth, I don't know what to do either."

"You should open a bakery," suggested Emily, munching on one of Mrs. Langley's buns. "Everyone needs to eat and these buns are delicious!"

"Now, that *is* an idea!" said Mrs. Langley.

"I could help!" said Isabel.

"That *would* be wonderful. But we'd need some money to start up a bakery," said Mr. Langley.

Matt and Emily looked at each other. Emily knew they were thinking the same thing. They couldn't take the gold back to the future anyway.

Why not give it to the Langleys to start their business?

"This is for you." Emily handed Mrs. Langley the bag of gold nuggets.

"We can't take this," said Mr. Langley. "The gold is yours."

"You have to take it," said Emily. "Please."

"I'll take it on one condition. We will use it to help all of us. You can all work in the bakery. Even you, Dan," said Mrs. Langley.

Dan's eyes lit up. "Thank you, ma'am. I would like that," he said.

"Now, you two go out and play." Mrs. Langley shooed Emily and Matt outside. "Isabel and I will tidy up, and Dan can have a nap. He looks like he needs one."

Emily and Matt ran to the back of the cabin. The ground was still muddy, so they sat on the magic sled.

"I'm glad we found gold and helped the Langleys, but I miss my family. I miss my room. I miss everything," said Emily.

"Me, too," said Matt. "I wish we could go home."

"Maybe we can! Look, Matt!" Emily pointed to the front of the sled.

Shimmery gold words were popping up.

You found real gold.
You made new friends.
You travelled far.
The trip now ends.

"Let's go!" sang Matt. He was about to rub the maple leaf.

"Wait!" said Emily. "Not yet. We have to leave the Langleys a note." Emily ripped a page out of her sketchbook and wrote:

Don't worry. We're ok. Thanks for everything. We'll never forget you.
Emily and Matt

She placed the note on a flat rock beside the sled, and put a pebble on it.

"Now!" she told Matt.

He rubbed the leaf three times fast.

In no time, they were back in the tower of Emily's house. They hopped off the sled.

"Look," said Matt. "It's twelve. Time stood still again—even though this adventure went on for days!"

Emily nodded. "It was hard to sled on all that ice and sail down those crazy rapids, but it was fun, too. And I'll miss the Langleys. Especially Isabel."

"I'll really miss Mrs. Langley's baking. Her cinnamon buns were the best."

"I could ask my mom to bake her famous gold-rush pie for us later," Emily suggested. "We could have some with milk."

"What's a gold-rush pie?" asked Matt.

"It's a layer of squished mosquitoes, covered with thick mud, and topped off with ground pebble icing. Mmm." Emily rolled her eyes. "It's—de-licious!"

MORE ABOUT...

After their adventure, Emily and Matt
wanted to know more about the gold rush.
Turn the page for their favourite facts.

Emily's Top Ten Facts

1. 22,000 people climbed the Chilkoot during the gold rush.

2. The Chilkoot Lock-Step is the name people gave to the slippery climb to the top.

That sounds like a goofy dance! —M.

3. Here is a trail hint from gold rush days: when your nose is bitterly cold, stuff both nostrils with fur, cotton, or wool.

4. Here is another trail hint: keep your sleeping bag clean. If it becomes inhabited, freeze the inhabitants out.

Inhabitants? You mean bugs! —M.

5. Samuel Steele was so good at keeping the peace and making sure people didn't steal or fight that there wasn't much crime in Dawson.

6. Some people got into arguments on the way to Dawson. Two best friends got so angry at each other while building their boat to sail on the Yukon that they split up. Instead of dividing everything, they ripped their bags in half and many of their supplies got ruined.

7. Two women sailed a boat down the Yukon River using underwear as sails.

8. Some of the boats that sailed on the Yukon were called *Seven-Come-Eleven*, *San Francisco*, and *Golden Horseshoe*.

9. About 100,000 people joined the gold rush. But only 30,000 people made it all the way to Dawson.

10. There's still gold in Dawson. In 2005, 1,134 kilograms (2,500 lbs) of gold were found. The gold was worth twenty million dollars.

Matt's Top Ten Facts

1. In 1897, part of a glacier melted on the Chilkoot Pass and water came crashing down on tents and houses. Three people died.

2. The people who came to find gold were called stampeders.

3. A photographer named E.A. Hegg took the most famous picture of the Klondike Gold Rush. The picture showed a long, slow line of people climbing up the Chilkoot Pass.

4. On the White Pass Trail from Skagway to Lake Bennett, over 3,000 pack animals died.

5. The "Three B's" is what the stampeders called the food people ate day after day: bacon, bread, and beans.

Mrs. Langley's "Three B's" were: big, buttery biscuits!
-E.

6. Dawson City flooded on May 28, 1898. Five feet of water covered the city and people needed boats to get around.

So that's why it was so muddy when we got there! -E.

7. Beginning on May 29, 1898, in only 48 hours, 7,124 boats landed in Dawson carrying 30 million pounds of food.

8. These were some of the boats: one-man rafts, three logs tied together, twenty-ton scows full of people and animals, canoes, packing boxes used as boats, outriggers, catamarans, and kayaks.

9. A stampeder named Belinda Mulrooney brought silk underwear, bolts of cotton cloth, and hot water bottles to the Klondike. When she sold them, she made a profit of six times the amount she paid for them.

10. Later, Belinda Mulrooney opened hotels and restaurants in Dawson and made even more money.

So You Want to Know...

FROM AUTHOR FRIEDA WISHINSKY

When I was writing this book my friends wanted to know more about the gold rush. I told them that *Crazy for Gold* is based on historical facts but most of the characters in the story (except Samuel Steele) came from my imagination. I also made up the movie that Emily and Matt saw about the gold rush, although there are real ones. Here are some more questions I answered.

What started the gold rush?

George Carmack, Skookum Jim, and Dawson Charlie discovered a bonanza of gold in the Klondike in August 1896. Almost a year later, two ships full of gold steamed into San Francisco harbour. When people learned that Yukon miners had found hundreds of kilograms of gold, they went crazy for gold. Word soon spread all around the continent and people flooded into Dawson to find gold too.

Why did people drop everything to join the gold rush, especially since it was so difficult to get there?

There were three main reasons. There was an economic depression at the time in North America and this looked like a great opportunity to get rich. The lure of adventure was another reason. And finally, many people were just not well-informed about how dangerous it all was going to be.

Samuel Steele sounds like an amazing man. Tell me more about him.

Steele had been a soldier since he was 15. He was one of the first to join the North West Mounted Police in 1873. He helped patrol the Canadian Pacific Railway while it was being built. His no-nonsense attitude and strict rules during the Klondike stampede made the difficult trip to Dawson safe, if not easy. He was also tall and impressive. One of Steele's colleagues described him as "erect as a pine tree and limber as a cat."

How did E.A. Hegg take those photographs of the gold rush stampeders in the middle of a blizzard?

Hegg hauled his camera and portable darkroom across the passes on a goat-drawn sled. Then he took his equipment on a poling boat called *Views of the Klondike Route* and took photographs of the wild river and rapids. Imagine travelling and photographing in those dark, dangerous, and slippery conditions!

Robert Service wrote the famous poem *The Cremation of Sam McGee* about the Klondike. How did that come about?

Robert Service was born in England, grew up in Scotland, and came to North America as a young man. He arrived in Dawson in 1906 when the gold rush was just about over. He wasn't looking for gold but adventure. In Dawson he worked in a bank and wrote poems. After he heard stories about the gold rush from old-timers in town, he wrote his famous poem. It became an immediate success.

What does "land of the midnight sun" mean?

The Yukon has a sub-arctic climate, which means it's cold and dark in the winter. Winter days are very short but summer days are very long. You can see the "midnight sun" from a high point in Dawson in late June.

How many miners actually found gold?

A few did, especially in the early days before 1897. The people who really made money were those who provided services for the gold seekers, like hotels, restaurants, stores, and bakeries.

What happened to Dawson after people stopped looking for gold?

At the height of the gold rush there were around 40,000 people in Dawson. In 1901, when gold rush fever had died down, the population fell to under 5,000. Today, only 2,000 people live in Dawson but in the summer tourist season, the population swells to over 60,000. Tourists rush to Dawson to visit the places where people once rushed to find gold.

Teacher Resource Guides now available online. Please visit our website at www.owlkidsbooks.com and click on Teacher Guides under Resources/Activities to download tips and ideas for using the series in the classroom.

The *Canadian Flyer Adventures* Series

#1 Beware, Pirates!

#2 Danger, Dinosaurs!

#3 Crazy for Gold

#4 Yikes, Vikings!

#5 Flying High!

#6 Pioneer Kids

#7 Hurry, Freedom

#8 A Whale Tale

#9 All Aboard!

**#10 Lost in
the Snow**

**#11 Far from
Home**

**#12 On
the Case**

**#13 Stop that
Stagecoach!**

**#14 SOS!
Titanic!**

**#15 Make
It Fair!**

**#16 Arctic
Storm**

**#17 Halifax
Explodes!**

More Praise for the Series

"[Emily and Matt] learn more than they ever could have from a history textbook. Every book in this new series promises to shed light on a different chapter of Canadian history."

~ *MONTREAL GAZETTE*

"Readers are in for a great adventure."

~ *EDMONTON'S CHILD*

"This series makes Canadian history fun, exciting and accessible."

~ *CHRONICLE HERALD (HALIFAX)*

About the Author

Frieda Wishinsky, a former teacher, is an award-winning picture- and chapter-book author, who has written many beloved and bestselling books for children. Frieda enjoys using humour and history in her work, while exploring new ways to tell a story. Her books have earned much critical praise, including a nomination for a Governor General's Award in 1999. In addition to the books in the *Canadian Flyer Adventures* series, Frieda has published *What's the Matter with Albert?*, *A Quest in Time*, and *Manya's Dream* with Maple Tree Press. Frieda lives in Toronto.

About the Illustrator

Gordon Dean Griffiths realized his love for drawing very early in life. At the age of 12, halfway through a comic book, Dean decided that he wanted to become a comic book artist and spent every spare minute of the next few years perfecting his art. In 1995 Dean illustrated his first children's book, *The Patchwork House*, written by Sally Fitz-Gibbon. Since then he has happily illustrated over a dozen other books for young people and is currently working on several more, including the *Canadian Flyer Adventures* series. Dean lives in Duncan, B.C.